Starting a Food Business

Step by Step Guide to Starting a Mobile, Concessions, Restaurant or Food Retail Business

Written by Susan Kilmer

www.secondchancespress.com

Introduction

I wanted to start off for thanking you for taking an interest in this book. The main purpose of ***Starting a Food Business: Step by Step Guide to Starting a Mobile, Concessions, Restaurant or Food Retail Business*** is to assist both the aspiring entrepreneur and seasoned business owner alike better understand business ownership and the steps needed to start a business including readiness, developing the business idea, appealing to customers, having sufficient capital and the business planning process.

The average individual knows through word of mouth and hearsay about the needed documentation to start a business, but few understand why they need to and the more important pieces of starting a small business. Even less know how to start and run a business properly including knowing how to be fully ready - time, effort and financially

My goal for this start up guide is for you to better understand what business ownership is like, the proper steps to start successfully and how you can minimize risks and sustain your business long term.

By the time you read the entire book, you will have a better understanding of the business planning process every business, big and small, will need to go through to manage the growth and operations of your business, how to start a business properly and what are the most important pieces of knowledge every business owner needs to remember throughout the lifespan of the business.

Enjoy!

Chapter 1

What is a Food Business?

In today's world, there is a new trend of street food connoisseurs invading the new hot spot, food truck, food festival or that little mobile food court on the corner. Although, food businesses are not a new concept for entrepreneurs and consumers, it is one of the preferred activities of the young adults and 20 something year olds. This generation is increasing year over year and will be if it already isn't, the biggest source of customers in the world population.

These food lovers are always on the hunt for the newest food and beverage mix, trendy hotspot or that iconic favorite that they can tell everyone they know about. All food businesses, whether a brick & mortar location, mobile business, booth or etc. must be aware not only of what the trends are but also must be aware of the legislation regarding food safety. As a business owner, you are ultimately responsible for ensuring that the food you are serving is well received and safe.

Food truck businesses are increasing in part due to the economic fluctuations the past several years. The sudden upsurge trend started off with consumers seeking inexpensive meal options that can be served in a short amount of time. Although in the beginning this had a slight effect on food based businesses that are brick and mortar based, restauranteurs were quick to add on food trucks as part of new revenue stream.

From an entrepreneurial standpoint, food trucks, mobile food business and booths/cart set ups have lower overhead expenses than restaurants and can easily relocate to pursue new revenue streams if needed.

From a consumer perspective, there is something amazing about not having to commute to get good food when the food will now come to you at a less expensive cost. There are a variety of options for those who want to start a food business:

- Restaurant
    - Full Service
    - Quick Service

- o   Delivery

- Retail Location

    - o   Shop

    - o   Farmers Market

    - o   Concessions

- Wholesale

    - o   Boutiques

    - o   Big Box Stores

But first, let us talk about the misconceptions of owning a business and the common mistakes aspiring entrepreneurs make before they even get their business off the ground.

These assumptions and mistakes are typically facts and suggestions everyone hears from their peers without really looking into what is being told. These suggestions lead to false assumptions about what having a business is like, what it will involve and how much money can be made. Most of the assumptions an aspiring entrepreneur has, is usually not realistic. Having unrealistic assumptions about having a business usually leads to the wrong strategies for their business which in turn creates uncontrollable problems that cause business failure.

Let's take a look at this false assumptions and common mistakes over the next couple of chapters.

Chapter 2

False Assumptions about Owning a Small Business

When individuals decide to start a small business or any business venture most often they start the process with assumptions ingrained in their brain about what the business environment is like without truly questioning what they hear or read. Having a belief without documented proof and research to backup that belief often leads the aspiring entrepreneur to make decisions and create strategies for their business that often times is completely wrong for their business and they are left wondering what happened.

I wanted to start off this book before we move on to the nitty gritty, listing out some of the common false beliefs people often have that typically lead to a lot of risks along the way. My hope is that if you or anyone who has any, some or all of these assumptions and beliefs listed below, that you have the capacity to change your mindset from assuming/believing to actually **_knowing._** Also, that you learn to research everything you hear or read and make a well thought out decision before you take any action regarding the needs of your business.

Some common <u>false assumptions and strategies</u> are:

1. **Relying heavily on others for answers and information without question.**

   Do not believe everything you read and hear. Instead, get into the habit of researching information and knowledge you obtain from others and understand **WHY** and *"connect the dots"* between facts and concepts. If you do not know why situations and facts are the way they are, then you will not have the ability to critically think through every situation you will come across in the life span of your business. If you have a business and you find yourself unsure of what you should be doing, why people aren't buying or you are standing there twiddling your thumbs confused, then you either have done something wrong, do not talk to your customers enough to know what they need and want, or you do not know enough about your business.

There is power in the knowledge YOU have and as a business owner you should KNOW your business and all of the influencers around it. If you have control and knowledge about every facet of your business, you will know how to handle most if not all situations that happen within your business life span.

2. **There are free grants and banks that will loan individuals money if they are starting a business.**

This is not true. You will need to contribute capital out of pocket to fund your business EVEN if you are looking for funding from other sources. Lenders, for example, will expect you to contribute at least 15-20% of your own funds (sometimes more than that) of your own funds into the business or they will automatically assume you have no faith in your business idea or that you do not have any financial responsibility or know-how.

Also, there are no truly *free grants* out there that will just give anyone funding. Most grants that do exist, which aren't many, are usually listed on grants.gov. These grants are usually geared towards educational institutions, nonprofits, specialized industries or emerging technologies within industries *for a reason.*

If you are the type of person that would not hand over your money to a random stranger just because they are starting their business, do not assume others will also including financial institutions. They are a business also. They cannot stay in business if they approved anyone walking through their doors asking for capital.

If you haven't found any grants you qualify for yet, it is because free grants for the general public typically do not exist and/or you do not meet the required stipulations provided by grants. Also, grants are never *free,* they always have stipulations attached and/or goals & requirements you have to achieve ahead of time before they fund your business.

3. **People will automatically love and know about your business when you officially launch.**

This is also not true. Remember, YOUR BUSINESS is the new entity that is coming into an already <u>established</u> marketplace. It is up to you to grab the attention of consumers who are already buying similar products/services to yours from other businesses that are already in existence and convey to them in a way that they understand and like; your business exists and has better value for them.

This isn't a *field of dreams* environment where if you build a business on a random street corner or create a website on the internet, that people will automatically trust you let alone know who you are. There are 14+ billion websites on the planet, for instance. How do you expect them to find you right away? It takes the proper marketing strategies and channels for them to hear about you and that takes time.

The more that you can do pre-grand opening/launch marketing ...the more time you save when you do officially open.

4. **Being resistant to the notion that your original business idea**

and concept will change and evolve.

Everyone who wants to start a business, typically falls in love with the concept that they want to start. So much so, that they are resistant to change any facet of it. The problem is, consumers will only buy from a business if that business offers something that is a solution to their problems and needs.

Having a business isn't primarily about what YOU want, it is primarily about providing what potential customers want. Their purchases are what will be responsible for what hopefully keeps you in business. If you don't focus on their needs, wants and preferences – they will not buy from you and you will not have the revenue to pay your expenses. At that point, you will no longer be in business.

You will need to put the customers first and their preferences change all the time. That is how trends and technology changes. As trends change, the marketplace you are in will change and your original business concept will have to evolve to keep in step with your changing industry.

If you do not change with it, you will get left behind and will ultimately have to shut down your business.

5. **There is one set magic formula for everyone who wants to start a business.**

This is definitely not true as well. Somewhere along the way in life, aspiring entrepreneurs grew up believing that there is some magical checklist in the sky that if followed, their business will be successful. This is destructive thinking

Although there are basic business principles and a basic flow, the start-up process for every single business, including ones in the same industry, <u>will be different.</u> There are <u>no</u> predesigned processes or timelines for your business because every business and vision within each business is different. The proper strategies and operations for your business all depend on what YOU want your business to look like and then you apply the basic principles into that.

Following a pre-designed checklist or any checklist will not make you successful, being aware of business principles, the external and influencers around and in your business and having the proper strategies for your business are the <u>minimum</u> you will need to put your business on the right path.

These are just some of the false and risky assumptions that I see aspiring entrepreneurs and current business owners have every single day. Having these risky assumptions are what make the business owners create strategies and decisions that negatively impact a business and they are left wondering where they went wrong.

The point of the 5 assumptions I listed above (and there are a lot more to this list) is that as the business owner it is your responsibility to make the right decisions for your business and you can't be a proper business owner if you are relying on anyone other than yourself to make your business successful. You have to plan ahead of time and take the logical steps to achieve the goals you want. You have to have patience and you have to think through every situation that you encounter. You have to make time for this

In Chapter 3, we will talk about the factors including the assumptions above that will prohibit any potential success you may have.

Chapter 3

Factors that Prohibit Success

Every year, millions of small businesses *fail* within any given year and an even higher number **never** get up and running for a variety of reasons:

1. **In it for the wrong reasons** including trying to fix financial bad habits and personal problems and situations that have nothing to do with business.

   You will have to spend money to start and operate your business, and if you have no capital and/or you are bad with finances, you will not have the capital you need to run a business successfully.

2. **Does not put in the required time, effort and capital needed for their business.**

   There is a saying in business, you will get what you give. If you put minimal effort into operating and planning strategies within your business, you will get minimal results and minimal return. You will need to make time and put money into the business constantly. You will also need to be willing to do this. This business will also need to become a priority to you, especially if it is your sole source of income.

3. **Has no understanding of customer needs of the marketplace business is in.**

The ability to stay in business will depend on the wiliness of consumers to not only purchase your products and/or services, but also that they will do it often enough that you earn enough revenue to cover your expenses plus an emergency cushion. Consumer purchases do not happen naturally – they purchase based on purpose and need. If a business provides a solution to a consumer's needs, more than likely that consumer will purchase from that particular business. It is important that you understand if your business is continuously fulfilling the needs of your customers as the constant fulfillment is the only way they will continue to purchase from your business.

The second your business stops providing what consumers need, they will stop buying from you and may tell other people about it. As a new business, it is important for you to continue the habit of gaining consumer feedback so that you can properly evaluate how your business is doing. You need to care about what your consumers think.

4. **No real differentiation in marketplace and product/service has no value offered to client.**

It is important for your business to not only provide value to potential customers but your business needs to provide it in a way that is different from your competition and everyone else, otherwise why will they buy from you (the new guy to the market place) when there are plenty of other businesses that they are already used to. Consumers purchase based on experience, value given and word-of-mouth. As a new business, it is your job to bring something different to the marketplace **and** has to be something that consumers are not getting from other similar businesses **and** it has to be something that they care about. If you operate your business with no real value or differentiation from your competitors, consumers will make decision based on convenience, price, location and word of mouth most of all. That is a tough sell.

5. **Poor management and strategy including trying to promote and sell product/service in the wrong channels and to the wrong people.**

It is virtually impossible physically and financially to sell to everyone 100% of the time, also you are going to come across 80% of the population who do not want or like the products you have to sell, and trying to convince them otherwise is a waste of your time. It is far easier to focus on the core group of people who would want to buy your products and services anyway, find where they are at and sell to them in those locations. Saves you time and saves you money. Also, it's easier to figure out what their patterns are if you only focus on a core group of people with similar lifestyles and patterns.

6. **Lack of proper planning and funding to start <u>and</u> operate a business. Lack of experience, education and training in industry and/or business development & management.** If a business owner does not have the proper funds, plans, training and experience to run a business; he or she will have a tough uphill battle to climb as they will not know what they should experience from day to day nor have the capacity to handle any situations that will happen.

The goal of a business owner besides serving the needs of its customers, but it also their goal to understand the patterns within their business and industry.   It is not normal to be confused daily as what you should be doing in your business. As I mentioned before, if you always find yourself confused and unsure, then you are doing something wrong.

Depending on the situation, you will need to either get more training, talk to your customers more...or research/plan/strategize your business more. Also, as I mentioned at the beginning of this guide, do not get accustomed to relying on others to make YOUR business successful. It is your business and YOU are the one responsible for it. You will have to take the self-initiative and make the proper choices in getting the training that you need.

Chapter 4

Longevity during a Down Economy

Around 2007, the economy was on a decline and as a result a lot of small businesses shut down and the unemployment rate was on the rise. This is not a new thing. Throughout history there have been many declines in the economic cycle, unemployment increases and businesses shutting down and throughout it all there have been some major corporations who were small businesses once, survive. What did they do to stay in business despite a down economy?

There are lists of hundreds of corporations that we all know including a lot that are on the Fortune 500 list that have been in business for many years that originally started as a small business during a down economy – whether at the beginning, during or at the tail end. The commonality between these lists of well-known companies is that they knew the needs of their customers at all stages. The ones who didn't, closed down.

At all stages, the business owner needs to have an ability to <u>gain insight into customer needs by engaging with them actively</u> to consistently prove the validity of their business concept and assess market potential and risks. The only way for customers to continue to purchase from your business, is only when your business continues to provide value and some benefit to them. That is the only reason why consumers buy, this fact has never changed.

You will need to implement strategies and systems within your business that will give you the ability to gain customer insight such as a mailing list, survey, basic sales conversations, etc. Point is that you must do it and you must do it often.

Chapter 5

Typical Business Start Up Process

Although there are basic business principles in business and there is a certain flow of when you should do things based on how the different pieces of the start-up process are connected, there is no standard pre-designed check list.

But to give each of you an idea of the flow of things you should be doing in your start up process and the general connection each step has, I have included a chart below.

Keep in mind: This process is not applicable to everyone as each process is different for each business. Which steps you do and the length of time you spend each one are dependent on your specific business. Understand basic business principles and apply what's necessary for your specific business situation.

The following chapters in a good portion of this guide, we will be covering a good majority of the 1st half of the aforementioned chart and will be going into more depth on the types of actions you typically will want to make, why and how each of these steps are also interconnected with the other.

Understand each of these steps completely, will give you a better understanding of not only how business works but it will also teach you over time how to critically assess every action that is taken in your business and what the proper strategies and steps are.

Chapter 6

Preparation (Step 1)

One must be have the proper components and resources in place before they start their business. First step in starting your business is to develop your business concept by brainstorming about:

- *Your time, financial and effort capacity*
- *Required entrepreneurial traits, business management skillset and industry experience*
- *Support system – Employees, Loved Ones, Partners and Network, etc.*

Why are each of these components important?

- Provides ability to understand internal and external influencers around your business

- Provides ability to develop <u>appropriate</u> and ongoing strategies for your business that will enable you to consistently reach the target customers that are willing to purchase your product or service.

- Provides ability to figure out the answers to common questions such as:

    - Where should I sell?

    - What price should I set my products/service at?

    - Do I have enough capital?

    - What do I write in my business plan?

    - How do I attract and retain the right customers?

    - What documentation do I need to have?

    - Etc.

Time and Effort Capacity

You will not only need to have a self-starter trait but you will also need to schedule recurring time to develop and evaluate strategies with the following areas within your business:

- Management and Operations
- Legal Issues

- Human Resources

- Marketing

- Web Development and Strategy

- Accounting

- Sales, etc.

Not doing so will create gaps and problems within your business. Since you are the business owner, there is no entity above you that will remind you to do each of these tasks, so you will need to take the initiative to plan accordingly and stay on top of what is going on within your business. You need to be data driven.

Skills, Entrepreneurial Traits and Industry Experience

Having the appropriate entrepreneurial traits, business management skillset and industry experience will make owning and operating a business, less of an uphill climb and battle. It will also provide you with:

- A greater understanding of the marketplace.

- The ability to identify customers, marketing strategies and opportunities for growth.

- Greater access to a ready list of contacts for your support system and network.

- Gives you more confidence as you have a better idea of what to expect and can foresee problems more clearly.

Trusted Support System

It can be lonely at the top as a business owner and it is so easy to think that you are the only ones that are having difficulty navigating through the waters of owning and operating a business but in fact, ALL business owners have trouble most if not all of the time. It is the nature of the task. What could ease your woes is putting together a support system to be there for you emotionally or for feedback purposes every now and then so that you can analyze your business strategies.

Having a third party opinion occasionally helps you evolve mentally and helps your business grow because neutral and objective third parties can identify gaps that you cannot see in your business.

There are different types of supportive people you can have from family, friends, network, your employees, etc. Each has a role that they can play in your business growth but the key is to make sure they are the *right* people for your business such as:

- **Employees:** The individuals that you will hire to work in your business play a vital role in the brand and perception potential and current customers will have of your business. Having the right employees who care about your goals, vision and objectives will be an asset to your business. Employees who are only there to self-service their own agenda, will not care about going above and beyond and providing great customer service to your clients.

- **Business Partner(s):** Having the right business partner for your business is crucial to how well your business will do during its lifespan. When finding the appropriate business partners you will need to identify the right people who can contribute financially but also experience to your business. This can help offset any gaps in your knowledge and skillset. Keep in mind, these need to be the <u>right</u> people for your business.

Business owners make the mistake of bringing in their family and friends as your business partner. What each of you need to remember is how they act personally, typically will be how they act in your business. One way you can protect yourself is to have a legally binding partnership agreement in place that outlines what each person is contributing, what will happen if one partner doesn't contribute equal effort, what will happen if one partner wants to leave, etc. Each of you cannot get hung up in the assumed glamour and fame and really need to talk about the operational pieces of the business before you launch. Time and time again I have seen businesses fail because there is a dysfunction between the business partners of the business.

- **Network:** You will need to put together a network of professionals in your industry or an advisory board that will be able to give you their unbiased and objective opinion on the strategies within your business. You can develop a network of people through contacts you meet within your industry, people you meet at Trade Association or Chambers of Commerce events. Point is, you cannot do this on your own and you do need industry opinions on things that you do and would like to do in your business.

- **Loved Ones:** Before you begin the process of starting your business, your family needs to be on board and be okay with you being gone more often than you use to. At times, your business will be more important and more of a priority than your business and they will have to be okay with that. Talk about possible scenarios with your spouse and other loved ones so they truly understand how important having this business will mean to you.

Chapter 7

Conceptualization and Research (Step 2)

Is this a business or a hobby?

After you have thoroughly investigated your preparedness emotionally, physically, time and willingness you will have to start defining the business idea in a more concrete fashion. Occasionally, an individual (this tends to happen in certain industries such as food based and creative backgrounds) gets told that what that should utilize their talents and start a business. Part of the problem with situations such as this and especially for those with artsy, creative or textile type of backgrounds. Typically individuals from these backgrounds have talents, sometimes it is not enough to have a sustainable business due to the fact that there isn't enough demand or potential customers will not purchase often enough for someone to cover expenses that will occur monthly.

There are several tests that one can use to really evaluate if their business idea is more of a hobby or if it has the potential to be a thriving and sustainable business. Some self-test questions you can ask yourself are:

- Is there <u>enough</u> of a market for it to build a sustainable income?

- Is the product/service a want or is it a need (solution to a problem)?

- Can it generate a profit?

- Is it scalable?

Creating a Business Concept

When you have a business idea, your goal in the very beginning is to develop it enough for you to have enough information to research its viability. You need to brainstorm and be aware of your products/service, competitors, target market, pricing, distribution channels and support system. Let's take a look at each of these components of a proper business concept below:

1. The product or service(s) being offered including identifying

features and end user benefits of each.

- Every single product or service should be a solution to a problem, fulfill a need or improve an existing solution not based on simply a want. Sustainability cannot exist without true value offered that exists beyond wants and features.

- Start by listing and describing each of your products or services i.e. attributes and know what purpose each item serves in solving a target customer's needs. How will it create value for them and how do they benefit?

- Remember, customers only buy products for **<u>end user benefits</u>** of product/service features and not the features itself!

- Think about all of the smart phones out there, especially the most popular one. You know which one I am referring to but in thinking about this particular brand and all of its reoccurring customers, what is perceived as? Think beyond functionality:

a. Personal Assistant/Organizer

b. Device that keeps you connected with loved ones

c. Filling In/Ego

d. Other

e. All of the above

The answer is **C. Fitting In / Ego**. The reasoning behind this answer is there are hundreds of smart phone brands out there that can do the same things: be a personal assistant/organizer, allows you to call/email/text loved ones, etc. but the difference between these brands and the most popular brand is that the 14-25 year old target market (core group of customers) buy based on what is most popular in itself because they themselves want to belong.

2. The identified target market(s) of your business

When it comes to brainstorming about your business concept you will also have to brainstorm about your identified target market, you need to start by thinking about who is most likely to buy what you have to sell. For example, think about the following scenario:

Two 30 year old women, both living in an upper class neighborhood with the same income, education, ethnicity but two different lifestyles: Soccer Mom vs. Business Professional.

When it comes to most products that they will purchase, will they acquire the same things around the same days, times, hours and quantities? More likely not. Although both women have similar profiles, their lifestyles are different. Lifestyles impact when they do things, what they are interested in and what their priorities are so as a business owner we can assume we can target and sell to everyone because it is physically and financially impossible to do so.

So instead of trying to assume the entire population will be interested in what you have to sell, it is far easier to figure out who would naturally be interested in the types of things you have to sell, understand their characteristics and where there typically are at, and communicate with them in ways they understand. This is far easier than trying to convince people to buy from you.

The **SOLE** existence of your business is to <u>provide your core group of customers with the products/services they need, at the price they expect in the areas/times that they want.</u>

REMEMBER the 80/20 Rule:

"20% of customers contribute to 80% of your sales"

(target customers)

The second goal of your business is to service your core group of customers (target market) well enough so that they become loyal customers. Loyal customers are very important because they are:

- Less sensitive to price changes
- They provide word-of-mouth and referrals
- Likely to purchase multiple or supplemental products/services

- Require less educating and selling time

- Makes your job easier and more satisfying

To create a profile of your potential target market, start by focusing on the core group of customers that will comprise most of your sales (**target customers**) and what you need to know about them:

- Their demographics and psychographics

- How they would typically use your product/service

- What influences their buying behaviors and purchasing patterns

- ***What do they value?*** Is it the features/benefits that you listed about your product/service?   <u>This requires speaking with potential customers to gather their insight and preferences.</u>

Knowing these facts about your potential target market will enable you to better shape your business strategies and operations in meeting their needs. It will also help shape your elevator pitch and messaging on all of your marketing material and website.

3. Potential competitors and their strengths/weaknesses

All business regardless of how unique they are have competitors. Both dircct and indirect. **Direct competitors** are businesses that operate similarly to you while **indirect competitors** are businesses that operate as an alternative to you.

When analyzing your competitors, at the very minimum you will need to find out things such as:

- Who are your competitors? Know at least 5 (a mix of indirect/direct)
- What are their products/services and how do they communicate the value of each?
- How do they promote and brand their business?
- Who are their target market(s)?
- How do they price their products/services?
- What are their revenue streams (distribution channels)?
- What their customers think about them and how you can capitalize on it

4. Appropriate distribution channel(s)

When identifying where you will earn your revenue (also known as revenue streams/distribution channels) you need to identify the appropriate places that your target market that you had profiled earlier can be found. It makes no sense to try and sell and market at locations where your target market will never be. Possible distribution channels are:

- Brick and Mortar

- Online / E-Commerce

- Mobile

- Farmer's Market

- Consignment

- Other retailers

- Sales Reps

- Others

- All of the above

The key to this is remember if your identified target market(s) can be found in those places and also if it is cost effective to do so.

5. A pricing strategy

You will need to figure out how to price your product or service. It is simply not enough to price without any logical reason why and it is just as bad to price just based on what your competitors are charging. You cannot price exactly the same as others because your business is different and your costs to operate is different. When pricing, you should consider factors such as:

- Generating enough revenue to create a profit. **This requires doing financial projections.**

- The value of your product/service i.e. expertise, delivery convenience, location, etc. **This requires knowing your product/service and what the unique selling proposition and value proposition is.**

- The criteria target customers use to make purchasing decisions. **This requires talking to them.**

- Competitors rates unless there is a strong differentiation then it should be comparable. **This requires performing a competitor analysis.**

6. Key partners and support system with outlined contributions

Do you have people in your life that will work with you, work for you, give you their industry perspective and support your decisions and time away? Ideally you will want to bring people into your business that are the right people who share the same vision and work ethic as you do. You also need to outline their contributions to your business on paper and hold them accountable for it. If they have actions that hurt your business, you will need to let them go.

Market Research // Feasibility (Viability Study)

After you have defined your business idea in a more concrete way, take the time to do thorough research to find out if your business idea will fit into the already established marketplace for your industry and product/service. If you find that your idea will not fit into the marketplace, do not proceed forward. You need to solve the hindrances that will cause your business idea to not operate successfully.

How and what you research depend on the questions YOU are looking for the answers to. Think about what it is you need to know to be fully confident that your idea will fit (or logically improve) and compete but <u>not</u> go against it and WHY. This is called a feasibility analysis.

Research can be direct research you perform yourself or data you collect from research performed by someone else. You can conduct research and analyze data through avenues such as:

- Surveys and focus groups you implement with your target market profile
- Market research companies (paid & fee based)
- Trade Journals and Associations
- Chambers of Commerce
- Tradeshows and Expos for your industry
- Research Databases (paid & fee based)
- Etc.

Chapter 8

Type of Food Businesses

There are many different types of food businesses including restaurants, bakeries, casual dining eateries, but also mobile food trucks, caterers, street carts, kiosks and manufacturers.

Depending on where the business is located, there will be different permits and licenses required to make the business happen. In all of the different types of food businesses listed above, the items or products being sold must be tested and perfected for safety before the business opens in order to minimize as many risks as possible.

Businesses that manufacture food that will ultimately be sold in retail stores will require a big investment upfront in order to minimize the variable costs per unit. The location and equipment for packaging the food items also must be the required permitting and regulatory requirements.

As mentioned at the beginning of this guide there are many types of food based businesses and we will only be talking in the following chapters about the most common ones:

- Restaurants
  - Full Service
  - Quick Service
  - Delivery Based

- Retail
  - Shops
  - Farmers Market
  - Concessions

- Wholesale
  - Boutiques
  - Retail Locations

Let's go into each of these a little further.

Chapter 9

Retail Food Locations

The most common food business to open up will be the retail food based businesses such as restaurants, casual dining eateries, farmers markets and concessions type of businesses.

There are also three common restaurant setups: **full service, quick service and delivery**. Opening a restaurant or food service business requires market research, business planning, sufficient funding, business and food based experience and determination as mentioned earlier in this guide. It also requires adhering to numerous legal and regulatory requirements at both the startup but also throughout the lifespan of the business.

- A **full service restaurant** is defined as a sit down retail location where food is served directly to the customers table. These type of food businesses also have the capabilities of serving alcohol, have casual dining services including take out, can also deliver and contract with entertainers to provide music or other forms of entertainment.

- A **quick service restaurant** is defined as a sit down or take out establishment that is known for its quick service i.e. fast food and typically has limited or nonexistent table services provided to customers.

- A **delivery service restaurant** is defined as a delivery only establishment that is only known for its delivery services to third party locations. Characteristics include the lack of ability for customers to be able to purchase food items on the restaurant premises. Quick services and full service restaurants may have delivery services available but a delivery service restaurant typically is characterized by the delivery service only feature.

When deciding to open a restaurant, an aspiring entrepreneur needs to really think about which type of establishment they want to be known for as each option mentioned above has different needs, requirements, set up obligations and funding amounts required. Full service restaurants typically have higher startup costs, overhead and operating expenses due to its more complicated and elevated nature.

Remember: the more moving pieces in the business, the more it requires to run it – people, funding and strategies.

Before opening your restaurant, you will need to be aware of several things:

- Zoning Laws

- How to negotiate a lease

- What business entity you want to incorporate into

- Required Permits and licenses

- Food Safety Regulations

- Have proper insurance

While in operation, you will need to be aware of things such as:

- Running and managing the restaurant

- Labor law regulations

- Payroll and tax requirements

There are also various other retail based food business such as farmers market booths and concession which has its own requirements.

Farmers markets and concessions type of businesses are a cost efficient way to test out your business concept on a smaller scale that will typically be within your financial means. It can also be a great way to introduce your concept to customers who care about specialty items. Also, farmers markets are a great way to be profitable due to its low overhead cost.

Some things to consider:

- Set up your booth in a way where it will be noticed amongst the other vendors. Use booth colors that are attractive and eye catching.
- Provide samples
- Be reasonably priced
- Don't over complicate your menu
- Have visuals on your menu board
- Leverage social media so your current customers know where you will be next

Chapter 10

Wholesale Food Businesses

With most food products available, there will be at least one well known company that will only sell their food brands through wholesale avenues. These days, most local and artisan food are becoming more common making it easier for aspiring entrepreneurs to break barriers to entry easily.

Building a wholesale food business is possible and with the right planning and preparation, you can build a successful business. Some things to think about:

- Have a niche or specialization

- Identify and profile the target market that more than likely will purchase what you have to sell and which retailers that are more likely to work with you.

- Obtain the necessary permits and licenses for your location. Keep in mind, different locations may have different requirements.

- Find the right commercial kitchen or manufacturing facility. In the beginning, renting a commercial kitchen will be enough and as you grow, you will be able to improve on the facility you will operate your business in.

- Be aware of your local, state and federal regulations regarding making any food products from your home kitchen.

- Have the appropriate and appealing packaging for your food product with the appropriate labeling and nutritional information and ingredient listing.

- Be sure to purchase your ingredients and supplies through wholesale as well to keep your costs to a minimum

- Create organized systems and processes that your business needs to stick with.

Chapter 11

What Type of Site Locations Will You Need

When starting a food business, a business owner needs to think about the type of facility they will need to operate their business out of. There are various types of site locations for a food based business including **owning a commercial kitchen, renting a commercial kitchen, working with a co-packer and even making products out of your own kitchen.**

Depending on the type of site location you want to start your business out of, each has its own legal and start up requirements. It is important to know the entirety of what you want to do.

In most places, food businesses are legally required to make their food products in a commercial kitchen that is licensed and approved by its local health and city agencies. Depending on the nature of your business and the perception you want customers to have about your products, will determine what type of facility you will need to obtain i.e. high end food products and brands will need to occupy high end business spaces.

Owning a Commercial Kitchen

The cost of owning and building a commercial kitchen will depend on what you want the kitchen to look like and have. It can range from $20k to an upwards of 120k depending on the size of the space, the complexity of the environment and the type of equipment it will utilize.

The main aspects of your kitchen will be the plumbing, ventilation and refrigeration equipment. Skimping on these areas of your kitchen including installation services will be detrimental and risky for your business. Ideally you want to occupy a space that has a commercial kitchen or use to have one as it will help you save money as it will have some of the items you will need, already in it.

Renting a Commercial Kitchen

Renting a commercial kitchen allows you to avoid the high expense of owning a commercial space. Various facilities throughout city locations will typically lease space or time slots to food businesses typically during the dates and times it isn't being used.

The cost of renting a commercial kitchen will vary from place to place but it can be anywhere from $100+ per hour depending on the payment structure and the types of equipment available for use. Keep in mind, although renting a commercial kitchen saves money, it does usually limit the time and days you can use the facility.

Using a Co-Packer

Many aspiring entrepreneurs at one point or another especially when they are too big to handle the volume they need to produce, make the decision of contracting with a co-packer. This is especially true because the co-packer tend to have the expertise in manufacturing food products at a better cost and at lower financial requirements. The key is you will need to find and select co-packer and it isn't always easy because there are many things to consider.

For you to be able to find the right co-packer, you will need to understand your own processes and costs. Having this knowledge will enable you to better manage the co-packer you will be working with in terms of the standards you want them to follow.

Be aware of following things:

- What type of service you specifically will need from them.
- Their qualifications, reviews from previous customer relationships they have had and their safety policies and standards they have for their own employees
- Are they completely open and honest with you
- How close are their facilities to you and your consumers, this will help eliminate a lot of the business costs you and your customers will incur.
- Do you know who their current clients are and have you talked to them already about the quality of service they have been getting?

Chapter 12

Business Planning and Projections (Step 3)

It is highly recommended that you do not try and write a business plan if you have not developed a solid business concept and performed the necessary research you need to determine if your business idea will be feasible or not as mentioned in previous chapters.

There is no purpose in writing a plan for a business that is not feasible and will not do well. In this chapter, we will be going over briefly the purpose of a business plan and what it consists of. If you need a more thorough explanation of what a business plan entails feel free and check out my other book: Small Business How to Guide to Writing a Business Plans Easily.

Although, writing a business plan is not a *must do*, but it is an integral part of the business start-up process. You should not write a business plan because you think you have to, write a business plan because you KNOW you NEED to and why. There has to be a reason why you want to write it, or it will be ineffective to your business. There are two main purposes why most people want to write a business plan: Internal and External.

Internal Purposes

- Internal roadmap of your business outlining what your vision for the business is, what you would like to do and how you plan on achieving your vision.
- Greater understanding of what you are doing within business through
- Increase likelihood of success

External Purposes

- Needed if trying to obtain financing.
- May be requested by third parties other than lenders
- Potential partners or collaborators

What is in a business plan?

- **Executive Summary** (First in plan but written last)

- **Business Description and Vision** – Company Background, history goals, objectives, mission and vision

- **Products and Services** – list of products/services, features, benefits, value added, pricing

- **Organization and Management** – management team, qualifications, special certifications

- **Marketing** – Industry trends, marketplace data, strategy of how your business will compete, target market, competitor analysis, etc.

- **Operating Plan** – location information, parking requirements, zoning, processes, systems etc.

- **Financial Information** – financial projections, costs, financial statements, sales forecasted, etc.

Why Write a Business Plan?

What you put into the plan is a description of the business YOU are wanting to create. Because your business plan is about the business you are trying to start and operate, it is not advisable to have a 3rd party write it as they do not know what it is YOU want to do and how YOU want to do it.

All of the required sections are pretty straightforward and are all items you need to think about and decide on. If you find yourself lost when writing a business plan, it is because you have not thought through your business concept thoroughly. Go back and further conceptualize your business idea as the different components of a developed business concept are similar to most of the sections of a business plan:

Business Concept Components	Business Plan Sections
Product Service ⟶	Products and Services
Target Market ⟶	Marketing
Competitor Analysis ⟶	Marketing
Pricing Strategy ⟶	Product and Services/Marketing
Distribution Channels ⟶	Marketing/Operational Plan
Cost Analysis ⟶	Financial Plan
Sales Forecast ⟶	Financial Plan
Key Partners and Support System ⟶	Organization & Management

How much will it cost to start and operate your business?

The startup and operational costs you may encounter depending on the nature of your business and what YOU want it to look like. Every business is different and thus the costs of every business and even ones in the same industry will be different.

When projecting your start up and operational costs make sure you factor in how it affects how much you can <u>realistically earn.</u> Good idea is to overestimate your expenses and underestimate your revenue. Always plan for worst case scenario.

Start- Up Costs include: Licenses/Permits, TI, Marketing, Equipment, Vehicles, Furniture, Utility Deposits, Merchant Services, Employee costs, insurance, professional fees, etc.

Operational Costs

- **Fixed Costs include:** Supplies, Utilities, Rent, Marketing/Advertising, etc.
- **Variable Costs include:** Costs that you incur in order to make & sell goods or provide a service i.e. ingredients, mileage etc.

Know your breakeven point!
Break-even point = fixed costs / (unit selling price - variable

Chapter 13

Identifying Funding Options (Step 4)

Do you have enough capital?

It is imperative that you have sufficient capital to not only start your business but also to maintain it. It isn't until you project your costs, will you know if you currently have enough funds out of pocket to make your business idea happen. There are several options if you do not have sufficient capital out of pocket. Obviously, the best choice would be to save until you can pay for most of your start up and operational expenses out of pocket to eliminate a lot of unnecessary debt in the beginning but we all know especially since the economic decline in 2007/2008 that is very difficult these days.

There are various types of financing and we will talk about the most common ones in this chapter:

Debt Financing

Debt financing is obtaining capital such as loans without giving up equity or ownership in the business to obtain it. Debt financing can come from financial institutions, lending institutions, non-traditional lenders.

The lending requirements vary between lending institutions and as mentioned in the beginning of this book, they do not give you money just because you are starting a business or because you are Mr. Nice Guy or Gal. They are a business themselves and one of the way earn revenue and stay in business is a client's ability to pay back the capital they borrowed plus the agreed upon interest.

Because lending institutions are dependent on a client's ability to pay, they implement qualification thresholds to eliminate a lot of the risks in lending. Typical lending considerations although vary between place to place, they all have typical minimums between all of them which are dependent on the capital amount you are requesting and other requirements. They will evaluate you based on the financial documents you submit as part of your loan application. The typical documents they will assess are:

- **Satisfactory FICO Score and Credit History**. Scores they typically have accepted were at minimums of 680-720 or higher. Some institutions have accepted lower credit scores of around 650 but it was more likely due to the individuals other financial documents surpassed the institution's expectations.

- **3 Years of most recent tax returns**. This is how they evaluate your income level interests to determine that if you had to return to the workforce, would your expected salary be sufficient to pay back a loan for the capital amount you want to request.

- **Collateral** – The higher capital amount you are requesting, the more they will expect you to have assets that are a 1 to 1 match in value. For example, if you are seeking $200K or more in capital, they will definitely expect you to have home equity of equal amount. The purpose is the financial institutions want their money back ASAP and if you default, they want to be able to liquidate assets you have quickly to get it.

- **Industry Experience** and **Business Plan.** They typically ask for your resume to show your industry experience as well as your business plan. These two sets of documents provide them with the opportunity to see if you have experience in the industry you would like to start a business in and do you have strong plan in place to make this business successful.

- Can contribute at least **25-30% out-of-pocket.** This is a set in stone standard for most financial institutions. This also helps them see that you have faith in your business idea.

- **Industry and growth trends.** They will look into the industry and see if it is a growing, declining or stagnant market. Sometimes the approval process isn't about you and your talents and plans, sometimes they will not approve someone because the industry they are getting into is declining and that scares financial institutions.

- **Written explanation** of amount seeking and a **breakdown of associated costs.** Financial institutions will often request a written statement of the amount you are seeking plus a breakdown of what you would like to use the funds for and any associate costs. They want to see what you will do with funds or if it was you just picking a number out of thin air.

Personal Financing

- Out-of-pocket: Minimum of 25-30%
- Family/Friends

Equity Financing

- Trusted Business Partner with capital to contribute
- Investor

Other

- Crowdfunding is a viable option dependent on the type of business you would like to start. Most business owners who use crowdfunding to fund their business and are unsuccessful at it is typically because they assume that they can just design a campaign without promoting it. Like the internet, there are millions of people on crowdfunding sites, so how will people find you if you do not talk about it or promote your campaign.

- Scale down/start small to where it fits your financial means is the most logical step if you cannot get outside funding for your business. There is nothing wrong with starting your business on a smaller scale so you don't incur any unnecessary expenses from the start. This also is a true benefit to people with minimal industry experience as starting small is less of a risk to obtain that experience. If an aspiring entrepreneur can make their concept work on a smaller scale, then they can grow into their ideal scenario instead of starting big and failing and most often times, not being able to adjust to the failure or adapt to it.

- *Free Grants?* As mentioned in the beginning of this guide, although there are free grants out there on legitimate sites such as www.grants.gov , very rarely if at all are these grants designed for the general public. Grants are made available because an economic development agency or governmental institution whether its federal, state or local has tasks within the community they need to solve and will occasionally recruit businesses to help them solve those economic issues. Thus grants are offered as a way to bring those specific businesses they need to solve those issues.

For example, a hair salon very rarely will qualify for a grant because most salons don't solve an economic need.

Chapter 14

What's Next?

After viability has been evaluated, next step would be to start the planning process i.e. developing a business plan to outline strategies to be used to launch business concept as described in previous chapters.

What makes a business feasible and viable is a business that has **the proper people, funding, business concept, plan and strategies in place before it starts.**

Without all of these things, you will not start off in the right direction and gaps will occur. If gaps and problems occur, be aware that it can snowball quickly and will require a strong financial capacity in order to fix it. More than likely if problems have snowballed, the business owner more than likely does not have financial capacity to fix it at any rate.

Chapter 15

Business Development (Step 5)

By now you have learned about what the small business landscape is like, how to prepare yourself, how to develop a business concept, obtaining funding, writing a business plan and maybe after all of that, the concept doesn't work no matter what you do. Sometimes it's not the concept itself but the avenue to which you start it.

Besides starting a small business independently, depending on your situation there may be more viable options to start your business in order to make it work. Other options besides starting an independent business are buying an existing independent business or buying a franchise.

Starting an Independent Business

This is the most common option but it can be the most risky. It is the most risky because you are essentially starting a business from scratch. But this also can be an advantage because you have the ability to create a business from the ground up according to what you envision.

Always be aware of the time, effort and financial requirements of having to create a proof of concept when consumers do not know your business exists and do not know who you are. There is no existing loyalty or trust. You should not fall victim to the field of dreams misconception to where if you build a business, automatically thinking they will come and purchase.

Independent businesses can have various set ups including brick & mortar, online, mobile, shared space, farmer's market, etc. It is much easier to deal with starting small and within your means, than to overshoot and fail.

Buying an Existing Business

The other avenue you pursue is buying an existing business especially if you aren't the creative and macro level thinker. When purchasing an existing business it gives you ownership of an existing product and/or service, the existing client base, existing suppliers and existing employees if applicable.

When buying an existing business, beware of the fact that the previous owners may not be entirely forthcoming about any operational and financial issues or that it may contain ineffective employees that you personally wouldn't hire or a tremendous amount of dissatisfied customers.

If you want to go this route, then be sure to do your research and be thorough in evaluating if their selling price is sufficient for what you will potentially be getting into.

Buying a Franchise

Buying an existing franchise is a lot like buying an existing independent business except the difference is that a franchise has a proven formula that you will have to follow. An existing independent business more than likely will just give you the clients and the equipment and maybe marketing materials, but very rarely they will give you the working formula to make it happen.

This is the bonus of a franchise. A franchise is designed to give you the formula for you to follow and most of the time if not all of the time the franchisor does not want you to deter from that.

They typically will charge you a set franchise fee to purchase the franchise location and it gives you the right to use the name of an established proof of concept and the ability to sell its products and/or services. The franchisor will also typically will charge you a royalty fee (typically between 3-12% of sales) on a recurring basis for continued support and the right to continue using the name.

The franchisor also typically dictates fees, locations to choose from, what they will provide you, what vendors you must buy your inventory from and what you can do within the business.

It is best if going the franchise route to pick a franchise that best fits your style and industry experience because the purchase does not automatically guarantee success and growth. It is up to you and your knowledge and efforts to maintain the formula the franchisor has designed to make the franchise successful.

Take away

The #1 question that all aspiring entrepreneurs ask is **How Do I Start My Business?** The answer is it depends on you. Having a business means that you as the owner are essentially dictating how the business starts and how it will operate and also as the owner you are the only person responsible for finding the right strategy to make it work. You can ask and research all you want, but you are the one that has to apply all of these principles to your specific business situation.

Before you decide to start your business and launch it, you should ask yourself several questions:

- Are you prepared?

- Do you have all the right resources and people in place?

- Do you know the industry and environment around your business?

- Do you have enough funding to start and operate your business?

- Do you have the right strategies to reach the core group of people who would be interested in my product/service?

If the answers to any or all of these questions are **no**, then you haven't prepared enough and you are not ready to launch. The more that you prepare ahead of time before obtaining sufficient documentation,

marketing materials and incurring any expenses the less risks you will start

with.